Philadelphia Eagles Trivia Quiz Book

500 Questions On All Things Green

Chris Bradshaw

Introduction

Think you know about the Philadelphia Eagles? Put your knowledge to the test with this selection of quizzes on all things green.

The book covers the whole history of the franchise, from the early days through to Doug Pederson's glorious Super Bowl-winning team and all points in between.

The biggest names in Eagles history are present and correct so look out for questions on Donovan McNabb, Carson Wentz, Jason Peters, Randall Cunningham, Mike Quick, Brent Celek and many, many more.

There are 500 questions in all covering running backs and receivers, coaches and quarterbacks, pass rushers and punters and much else besides.

Each quiz contains a selection of 20 questions and is either a mixed bag of pot luck testers or is centered on a specific category such as the 1990s or defense.

There are easy, medium and hard questions offering something for Philadelphia novices as well as Eagles experts.

You'll find the answers to each quiz below the bottom of the following quiz. For example, the answers to Quiz 1: Super Bowl LII, are underneath Quiz 2: Pot Luck. The only exception is Quiz 25: Anagrams. The answers to these can be found under the Quiz 1 questions.

All statistics refer to the regular season only unless otherwise stated.

We hope you enjoy the Philadelphia Eagles Trivia Quiz Book.

October 2021 Update

This latest edition of the Philadelphia Eagles Trivia Quiz Book has been fully revised and updated. All statistics and records are now accurate to the start of the 2021 season.

You'll also find 100 brand-new trivia teasers to test your knowledge on all things Eagles. These are at the back of the book in the Bonus Questions section. As usual, you'll find the answers to each quiz at the bottom of the quiz that follows.

Good luck!

About the Author

Chris Bradshaw has written more than 30 quiz books including titles for Britain's biggest selling daily newspaper, The Sun, and The Times (of London).

In addition to the NFL, he has written extensively on soccer, cricket, darts and poker.

He lives in Birmingham, England and has been following the NFL for over 30 years.

Acknowledgements

Many thanks to Ken and Veronica Bradshaw, Heidi Grant, Steph, James, Ben and Will Roe and Graham Nash.

Front cover image created by **headfuzz by grimboid**. Check out his collection of sport, movie, music and TV posters at: https://www.etsy.com/shop/headfuzzbygrimboid

CONTENTS

Quiz 1: Super Bowl LII

1. Which team did the Eagles face in Super Bowl LII?

2. What was final score in the game?

3. Who was named the game's Most Valuable Player?

4. Super Bowl LII was hosted in which city?

5. Who scored Philadelphia's only rushing touchdown in Super Bowl LII?

6. Who scored the first points of Super Bowl LII?

7. Whose strip sack late in the game help stifle any potential comeback?

8. Nick Foles became the first player in Super Bowl history to throw and catch a touchdown pass. Who threw the historic pass to the Philly quarterback?

9. Who caught a 34-yard pass to score the game's only first quarter touchdown?

10. Who was the only Eagle with 100 receiving yards in Super Bowl LII?

11. True or false – The Eagles never trailed during the whole of Super Bowl LII?

12. Which TV commentary duo were in the booth for Super Bowl LII?

13. Whose 11-yard touchdown catch with 2.21 remaining gave the Eagles a five-point lead?

14. What role was performed by a man called Hershel Woodrow 'Woody' Williams at Super Bowl LII?

15. True or false – The Eagles started Super Bowl LII as a 5.5-point underdog?

16. Who was the referee at Super Bowl LII?

17. Which singer sang the National Anthem prior to the game?

18. Which singer headlined the half-time show at Super Bowl LII?

19. How many times was Nick Foles sacked during Super Bowl LII? a) none b) once c) twice

20. How many yards did the Eagles defense give up in Super Bowl LII? a) 413 b) 513 c) 613

Quiz 25: Answers

1. Nick Foles 2. Doug Pederson 3. Darren Sproles 4. Carson Wentz 5. Donovan McNabb 6. Zach Ertz 7. LeSean McCoy 8. Brent Celek 9. Fletcher Cox 10. Andy Reid 11. Brian Dawkins 12. Ron Jaworski 13. Jason Peters 14. Trent Cole 15. Brian Westbrook 16. Harold Carmichael 17. DeSean Jackson 18. David Akers 19. Clean Jokes 20. Nelson Agholor

Quiz 2: Pot Luck

1. Before taking over in Philadelphia, head coach Doug Pederson was the offensive coordinator of which team?

2. Which long-time Eagles defensive back was elected to the 2018 Pro Football Hall of Fame class?

3. 'The Minister of Defense' was the nickname of which Eagles great?

4. What number jersey did quarterback Carson Wentz wear?

5. Before Carson Wentz, who was the last quarterback selected by the Eagles in the first round of the NFL Draft?

6. In March 2013, which 34-year-old became the youngest general manager in the NFL after taking the role with the Eagles?

7. The #99 jersey has been retired in honor of which player?

8. In 1994, who became the owner of the Eagles?

9. Which quarterback did the Eagles trade to the Vikings in 2016 in exchange for first and fourth-round draft picks?

10. The Eagles converted a miracle fourth and 26 in the closing stages of a 2004 playoff game against which team?

11. Which receiver caught the 28-yard pass on that famous play?

12. 'Jaws' was the nickname of which long-time Eagles quarterback?

13. Which two members of the 2017 World Championship-winning team won Super Bowl rings with the Patriots a year previously?

14. Who holds the franchise record for the most rushing yards in playoff games?

15. Which versatile Eagle is the only player in NFL history with 30 receiving touchdowns, 20 rushing touchdowns and at least one kickoff and punt return touchdown?

16. What number jersey did running back Ricky Watters wear?

17. Who is the only Eagles head coach to win the division title in his first season in charge?

18. Former receiver Nelson Agholor was born in which African country?

19. What was the name of the area of Veterans Stadium that was home to some of the team's most vociferous fans? a) 700 Level b) 800 Level c) 900 Level

20. The longest winning streak in franchise history ran for how many games? a) seven b) eight c) nine

Quiz 1: Answers

1. New England 2. Eagles 41-33 3. Nick Foles 4. Minneapolis 5. LeGarrette Blount 6. Jake Elliott 7. Brandon Graham 8. Trey Burton 9. Alshon Jeffery 10. Corey Clement 11. False 12. Al Michaels and Cris Collinsworth 13. Zach Ertz 14. He did the coin toss 15. True 16. Gene Steratore 17. Pink 18. Justin Timberlake 19. a) None 20. c) 613

Quiz 3: 2017 World Champions

1. What was the team's 2017 regular season record?

2. The Eagles squeaked past which team 15-10 in the Divisional Round of the playoffs?

3. Philadelphia routed which team in the NFC Championship Game to reach Super Bowl LII?

4. What was the score in that NFC Championship mismatch?

5. Quarterback Carson Wentz suffered a season-ending injury during a 43-35 win over which team?

6. Which long-time NFL quarterback was Philadelphia's offensive coordinator in 2017?

7. Who was the team's defensive coordinator in 2017?

8. The Eagles routed which highly rated defense in week nine, winning 51-23?

9. With 74 catches, who led the team in receiving in 2017?

10. The Eagles won how many straight games during the middle of the season?

11. True or false – The Eagles were underdogs in all three playoff games en route to their World Championship title?

12. Which defensive lineman led the team in sacks in 2017 with 9.5?

13. The Eagles sent a fourth-round draft pick to which team to acquire the services of running back Jay Ajayi?

14. What was the only AFC team to defeat the Eagles in 2017?

15. True or false – No Eagle rushed for over 1,000 yards or had 1,000 receiving yards during the 2017 regular season?

16. The Eagles offense was shut out in week 17 by which NFC rival?

17. Who were the two defensive members of the 2017 roster elected to the Pro Bowl?

18. Who were the four offensive players elected to the Pro Bowl?

19. How many points did the Eagles score during the 2017 regular season? a) 437 b) 447 c) 457

20. How many points did the Eagles give up during the 2017 regular season? a) 295 b) 305 c) 315

Quiz 2: Answers

1. Kansas City 2. Brian Dawkins 3. Reggie White 4. #11 5. Donovan McNabb 6. Howie Roseman 7. Jerome Brown 8. Jeffrey Lurie 9. Sam Bradford 10. Green Bay 11. Freddie Mitchell 12. Ron Jaworski 13. Chris Long and LeGarrette Blount 14. Brian Westbrook 15. Darren Sproles 16. #32 17. Chip Kelly 18. Nigeria 19. a) 700 Level 20. c) Nine

Quiz 4: Pot Luck

1. What color jerseys did the Eagles wear in Super Bowl LII?

2. Who is the winningest coach in team history?

3. Which Eagle led the NFL in sacks in 1992?

4. How many sacks did he record in that record-breaking 1992 season?

5. What number jersey did versatile runner, receiver and returner Darren Sproles wear?

6. Which member of the Eagles 2017 roster has a brother who plays linebacker for the Vikings?

7. Which team did the Eagles face in a controversial 1989 match up known as 'The Bounty Bowl'?

8. Which legendary Eagles offensive lineman started his NFL career in 2004 as an undrafted tight end with the Buffalo Bills?

9. Coach Doug Pederson won a Super Bowl ring as a player with which team?

10. Which quarterback was nicknamed 'The Polish Rifle'?

11. Who was the last coach before Doug Pederson to lead the team to a playoff win?

12. In 2009, which Eagle became the first player in NFL history to be voted to the Pro Bowl in two different positions in the same season?

13. True or false – Since 1995, the Eagles have made the playoffs more times than any other NFC team?

14. In 2011, for the first time in team history, the Eagles had three receivers with over 800 receiving yards. Which three?

15. Who won more games as the Eagles head coach – Buddy Ryan or Rich Kotite?

16. Which long-time Eagles rusher was the running backs coach on the 2017 Super Bowl-winning team?

17. Throughout their history have the Eagles scored more rushing or receiving touchdowns?

18. True or false – Since the 1970 NFL/AFL merger the Eagles have always been in the NFC East?

19. The Eagles longest home losing streak stretches to how many games? a) eight b) nine c) ten

20. What is the seating capacity of Lincoln Financial Field? a) 65,597 b) 67,479 c) 69,879

Quiz 3: Answers

1. 13-3 2. Atlanta 3. Minnesota 4. Eagles 38-7 Vikings 5. LA Rams 6. Frank Reich 7. Jim Schwartz 8. Denver 9. Zach Ertz 10. Nine 11. True 12. Brandon Graham 13. Miami 14. Kansas City 15. True 16. Dallas 17. Fletcher Cox and Malcolm Jenkins 18. Brandon Brooks, Zach Ertz, Lane Johnson and Carson Wentz 19. c) 457 20. a) 295

Quiz 5: Quarterbacks

1. With 32,873 yards, who is Philadelphia's all-time leading passer?

2. What number jersey did Randall Cunningham wear?

3. With which pick of the 2016 NFL Draft did the Eagles select Carson Wentz?

4. In November 2013, Nick Foles tied an NFL record after throwing seven touchdown passes against which team?

5. Who holds the franchise record for the most touchdown passes in a single season?

6. The longest pass in team history was a 99-yard touchdown thrown by which quarterback?

7. The Eagles signed Nick Foles for a second time in 2017 after he was released by which team?

8. Donovan McNabb holds the record for the most 300-yard passing games in team history. Who is second on that list?

9. Which quarterback had a better yards-per-rush average – Randall Cunningham or Michael Vick?

10. Who holds the team record for the most passing attempts in a season?

11. Carson Wentz played college ball at which school?

12. Who was the first Eagles quarterback to throw for 4,000 yards in a single regular season?

13. Who is the only Eagles quarterback to have had his jersey number retired?

14. Donovan McNabb is the quarterback with the most career wins in team history. Who comes next on that list?

15. Who are the four Philadelphia quarterbacks to have thrown 30 or more touchdown passes in a single regular season?

16. Which former Super Bowl winner was 9-3 as a starter during a spell with the Eagles that ran from 1990 through to 1992?

17. Whose 151 interceptions are the most in team history?

18. Of quarterbacks with at least 500 attempts who has the best completion percentage?

19. Before Carson Wentz in 2016, who was the last Eagles quarterback to start all 16 games in a regular season? a) Sam Bradford b) Randall Cunningham c) Donovan McNabb

20. In 2013, Nick Foles attempted 317 passes. How many of them were intercepted? a) 2 b) 4 c) 6

Quiz 4: Answers

1. Green 2. Andy Reid 3. Clyde Simmons 4. 19 sacks 5. #43 6. Mychal Kendricks 7. Dallas 8. Jason Peters 9. Green Bay 10. Ron Jaworski 11. Andy Reid 12. DeSean Jackson 13. False 14. DeSean Jackson, Jeremy Maclin and Brent Celek 15. Buddy Ryan 16. Duce Staley 17. Receiving 18. True 19. b) Nine 20. c) 69,879

Quiz 6: Pot Luck

1. 'Shady' was the nickname of which Eagles running back?

2. What number jersey did tight end Brent Celek wear?

3. Before Nelson Agholor in 2015, who was the last wide receiver selected by the Eagles in the first round of the NFL Draft?

4. Which Eagle, drafted first overall in 1949, played both offense and defense throughout his legendary 14-year career?

5. Which member of the Super Bowl-winning team donated all his 2017 salary to charity?

6. In November 2010, the Eagles were on the right end of a wild 59-28 scoreline against which team?

7. Which Eagles linebacker, who was picked in the third round of the 2015 NFL Draft, had 12 takeaways in his first 25 games in the league?

8. 'Weapon X' was the nickname of which former Eagles defensive star?

9. Which fearsome defensive duo combined for a team record 33 sacks in 1992?

10. Since their foundation do the Eagles have an overall winning or losing regular season record?

11. True or false – The Eagles have never lost on Thanksgiving Day?

12. Who holds the record for the most games played by a quarterback in franchise history?

13. Which DB became the first Eagle in over a decade to win the NFC Defensive Player of the Week Award after recording eight tackles and a pick six against the 49ers in October 2017?

14. Which future Super Bowl winner was the head coach of the Eagles from 1976 through to 1982?

15. True or false – Trent Cole is a cousin of two-time NBA champion Norris Cole?

16. Which defensive lineman scored his second career touchdown when he returned a Kirk Cousins fumble for a score in the 2017 opener?

17. What number jersey is worn by star offensive lineman Jason Kelce?

18. What is the name of the Philadelphia fight song which is played after touchdowns?

19. What color throwback jerseys did the Eagles wear in their 75th Anniversary game against Detroit? a) red and white b) green and red c) yellow and blue

20. How many of the Eagles 53-man Super Bowl LII roster had previously appeared in the big game? a) six b) eight c) ten

Quiz 5: Answers

1. Donovan McNabb 2. #12 3. Second 4. Washington 5. Carson Wentz 6. Ron Jaworski 7. Kansas City 8. Randall Cunningham 9. Michael Vick 10. Carson Wentz 11. North Dakota State 12. Carson Wentz 13. Donovan McNabb 14. Ron Jaworski 15. Carson Wentz, Sonny Jurgensen, Randall Cunningham and Donovan McNabb 16. Jim McMahon 17. Ron Jaworski 18. Sam Bradford 19. c) Donovan McNabb 20. a) 2

Quiz 7: Rushers

1. With 6,792 yards, who is the leading rusher in franchise history?

2. In 1996, which back set the team record for the most rushing attempts with 353?

3. Which two-time Pro Bowler rushed for 5,995 yards between 2002 and 2009?

4. Which rusher's 6,538 yards between 1977 and 1984 are good for second on the all-time list?

5. Whose 91-yard touchdown run against the Falcons in 1994 is the longest in team history?

6. Who was the only Eagles back to rush for over 100 yards in a game during the 2017 regular season?

7. LeSean McCoy rushed for a franchise record 217 yards in a 2013 game against which NFC North team?

8. True or false – In a 1939 game against Chicago the Eagles rushed for minus 39 yards?

9. Of Eagles players with over 400 attempts, who has the best yards per rush average?

10. In a 2000 game against Dallas, who became only the second Eagles back to rush for 200 yards in a game?

11. Who was the last Eagles running back to lead the NFL in rushing?

12. Which Eagles full back was named a first-team All-Pro in 2009?

13. True or false – No Eagles rookie has ever rushed for 1,000 yards?

14. Which alliteratively named back's 178 yards against the Panthers in November 2012 are the most by an Eagles rookie in a single game?

15. Who holds the team record for the most 100-yard rushing games in a single regular season?

16. Who was the last running back selected by the Eagles in the first round of the NFL Draft? (clue – it was 1986)

17. Whose 71-yard scamper against the Cowboys was the longest run in the 2017 World Championship season?

18. Who holds the record for the most rushing touchdowns in franchise history with 69 scores between 1944 and 1951?

19. Who led the team in regular season rushing touchdowns during the 2017 World Championship run? a) Jay Ajayi b) LeGarrette Blount c) Corey Clement

20. In 2011, LeSean McCoy set the franchise record for the most rushing touchdowns in a season with how many? a) 16 b) 17 c) 18

Quiz 6: Answers

1. LeSean McCoy 2. #87 3. Jeremy Maclin 4. Chuck Bednarik 5. Chris Long 6. Washington 7. Jordan Hicks 8. Brian Dawkins 9. Reggie White and Clyde Simmons 10. Losing 11. False – they're 6-1 12. Donovan McNabb 13. Jalen Mills 14. Dick Vermeil 15. True 16. Fletcher Cox 17. #62 18. Fly, Eagles, Fly 19. c) Yellow and blue 20. a) Six

Quiz 8: Pot Luck

1. The Eagles signed star wide receiver Alshon Jeffery after he was released by which team?

2. Who are the two Eagles head coaches to have steered the team to 13 wins in a single regular season?

3. Which running back holds the record for the most yards from scrimmage in team history?

4. Which rookie defensive lineman returned a fumble 23 yards for a touchdown in a 19-10 win over Oakland on Christmas Day 2017?

5. Which sturdy offensive lineman was the only player to feature in all 1,133 offensive snaps during the 2016 season?

6. Which two Eagles quarterbacks are the only players to pass for over 3,000 yards and rush for over 500 yards in back-to-back seasons?

7. Who caught Carson Wentz's first career touchdown pass against the Browns in 2016?

8. Which former Eagles defensive lineman appears on Twitter using the moniker @MrGetFlee99?

9. Did Chip Kelly have an overall winning or losing record as Eagles head coach?

10. In 1978, the Eagles played their first preseason game on foreign soil. Which city hosted that game?

11. Which Hall of Fame offensive lineman was the Eagles head coach from 1973 through to 1975?

12. True or false – The 74 combined points in Super Bowl LII was the most in the history of the Super Bowl?

13. What was the unfortunate nickname of defensive back Izel Jenkins?

14. In 2016, which defensive lineman became the first Eagle since 2008 to play snaps on offense and defense in the same game?

15. Nine players from which team were knocked out of a 1990 contest against the Eagles that became known as the 'Body Bag Game'?

16. Which future Philadelphia running back was an emergency quarterback in that game after the Eagles knocked out the opposition's starter and back-up quarterbacks?

17. The Eagles won their second NFL Championship title in 1949 after defeating which team 14-0?

18. Which long snapper appeared in 162 straight games between 2006 and 2016?

19. The team's longest road winning streak runs to how many games? a) seven b) eight c) nine

20. Nick Foles set the team record for the most passing attempts in a single game after throwing how many times against the Cardinals in 2014? a) 58 b) 60 c) 62

Quiz 7: Answers

1. LeSean McCoy 2. Ricky Watters 3. Brian Westbrook 4. Wilbert Montgomery 5. Herschel Walker 6. LeGarrette Blount 7. Detroit 8. True 9. Randall Cunningham 10. Duce Staley 11. LeSean McCoy 12. Leonard Weaver 13. True 14. Bryce Brown 15. Wilbert Montgomery 16. Keith Byars 17. Jay Ajayi 18. Steve Van Buren 19. c) Corey Clement 20. b) 17

Quiz 9: Receivers

1. Who caught a record 589 passes between 1971 and 1983?

2. Whose 99-yard touchdown grab against the Falcons in 1985 is the longest in team history?

3. Who holds the team record for the most touchdown receptions in a season after grabbing 14 in 2004?

4. Which tight end's 15 catches against Washington in December 2014 are the most in a single game in team history?

5. Who holds the record for the most career receptions by an Eagles running back?

6. Which receiver enjoyed a 221-yard receiving game against Detroit in 2007?

7. The Eagles used the 20th pick of the 2015 NFL Draft to select which wide receiver?

8. Who holds the franchise record for the most receiving yards in a single season?

9. Which receiver caught 87 and 89-yard touchdowns against Dallas and Atlanta in his rookie year in 2006?

10. Who caught a team record four touchdown passes in a 1996 win over Miami?

11. Who amassed more receiving yards during his time in Philadelphia – Jeremy Maclin or DeSean Jackson?

12. The Eagles signed controversial receiver Terrell Owens after a trade with which team?

13. Which tight end's 81 receptions in 1988 are the most in team history by an Eagles rookie?

14. Zach Ertz and Nelson Agholor were two of three Eagles receivers to enjoy a 100-yard receiving game in the 2017 regular season. Who was the third?

15. In 1972, which Eagles receiver led the NFL in receptions and yards (62-1,048)?

16. Who holds the team record for the most catches in a single season?

17. In 1990, which receiver caught nine touchdown passes, the most by an Eagles rookie?

18. Whose 7,412 receiving yards between 1956 and 1966 are the most by an Eagles tight end?

19. Who holds the franchise record for the most 100-yard receiving games in a season? a) Irving Fryar b) Harold Jackson c) Terrell Owens

20. Who holds the record for the most career 150-yard receiving games in team history? a) DeSean Jackson b) Terrell Owens c) Mike Quick

Quiz 8: Answers

1. Chicago 2. Andy Reid and Doug Pederson 3. Brian Westbrook 4. Derek Barnett 5. Jason Kelce 6. Randall Cunningham and Michael Vick 7. Jordan Matthews 8. Vinny Curry 9. Winning 10. Mexico City 11. Mike McCormack 12. False 13. Toast 14. Beau Allen 15. Washington 16. Brian Mitchell 17. L.A. Rams 18. Jon Dorenbos 19. c) Nine 20. c) 62

Quiz 10: Pot Luck

1. What number jersey did star quarterback Donovan McNabb wear?

2. Who is the play-by-play announcer on Eagles radio broadcasts?

3. Whose #20 jersey was retired in a ceremony against the Giants in September 2012?

4. Who was the only Eagle named on the NFL All-Decade Team of the 80s?

5. Which former Eagle wrote a book called, 'Lay It Down: How Letting Go Brings Out Your Best'?

6. Do the Eagles have a winning or losing record in overtime games?

7. Which running back rushed for two touchdowns and caught two more in a 48-20 win over Arizona in 2008?

8. True or false – Former Eagles defensive back Jaylen Watkins is the brother of Bills, Chiefs and Ravens wide receiver Sammy Watkins?

9. Which defensive back, who spent eight seasons in Philadelphia between 1996 and 2003 is now an Executive Vice President with the NFL?

10. Since 1982, who are the three Eagles to have recorded four sacks and three interceptions in the same season?

11. Which former AFC Rookie of the Year was 1-2 as starting quarterback in a brief spell in Philadelphia in 2011?

12. 'The Ultimate Weapon' was the nickname of which Eagles quarterback?

13. Which Eagles defensive star is the owner of a business selling bow ties called Rock Avenue?

14. True or false – in 1939 the Eagles were involved in a game that finished 0-0?

15. Which head coach had a 36-28 win-loss record in his spell with the Eagles between 1991 and 1994?

16. What number jersey did controversial receiver Terrell Owens wear?

17. Which former running back was named the team's assistant head coach in February 2018?

18. The Eagles acquired the services of quarterback Ron Jaworski following a trade with which team?

19. What was multiple Pro Bowl offensive lineman Tra Thomas's given first name? a) George b) Thomas c) William

20. How much did The Linc cost to build? a) $312m b) $412m c) $512m

Quiz 9: Answers

1. Harold Carmichael 2. Mike Quick 3. Terrell Owens 4. Zach Ertz 5. Brian Westbrook 6. Kevin Curtis 7. Nelson Agholor 8. Mike Quick 9. Hank Baskett 10. Irving Fryar 11. DeSean Jackson 12. San Francisco 13. Keith Jackson 14. Torrey Smith 15. Harold Jackson 16. Zach Ertz 17. Calvin Williams 18. Pete Retzlaff 19. c) Terrell Owens 20. a) DeSean Jackson

Quiz 11: Defense

1. Who is the team's all-time leader in sacks?

2. Who returned an interception 50 yards for a touchdown to open the scoring for the Eagles in the 2017 NFC Championship game?

3. The Eagles used the 14th overall pick of the 2017 NFL Draft to select which defensive end?

4. Which defensive tackle returned a fumble 98 yards for a touchdown against the 49ers in September 2006?

5. 'The Axe Man' was the nickname of which fearsome linebacker who had three spells in Philadelphia between 1998 and 2009?

6. Whose 183 regular season appearances between 1996 and 2008 are the most by a defensive player in team history?

7. Who are the two Eagles cornerbacks to be elected to the Pro Bowl five times?

8. Who returned a Tom Brady interception 99 yards for a touchdown against the Patriots in December 2015?

9. Which Eagles great was tragically killed in a car crash in Florida in June 1992?

10. Whose 39.5 sacks between 1991 and 1997 were at that time, the most by an Eagles interior defensive lineman?

11. Which 2005 fifth round draft pick went on to record 85.5 sacks, the second most in team history?

12. Reggie White is one of two Eagles to have recorded three sacks in a game three times in the same season. Who is the other?

13. Which Eagles defensive back set an NFL record in 1993 after returning four interceptions for touchdowns?

14. Which pair of Eagles defensive backs combined for a 104-yard interception return touchdown against Dallas in 1996?

15. Which pair of Eagles recorded more than one multi-sack game during the 2017 season?

16. Which defensive tackle was voted to his sixth straight Pro Bowl in 2020?

17. Which linebacker, who played in Philly from 1986 until 1993, holds the team record for the most fumble return touchdowns?

18. Which alliteratively named defensive back, who has the same name as a former Democratic Presidential candidate, holds the team record for the most interceptions in a single season with 11?

19. Who holds the record for the most sacks in a single season? a) Jason Babin b) Clyde Simmons c) Reggie White

20. How many sacks did he record to set that record? a) 20 b) 21 c) 22

Quiz 10: Answers

1. #5 2. Merrill Reese 3. Brian Dawkins 4. Reggie White 5. Randall Cunningham 6. Losing 7. Brian Westbrook 8. True 9. Troy Vincent 10. Seth Joyner, William Thomas and Mychal Kendricks 11. Vince Young 12. Randall Cunningham 13. Malcolm Jenkins 14. True 15. Rich Kotite 16. #81 17. Duce Staley 18. L.A. Rams 19. c) William 20. c) $512m

Quiz 12: Pot Luck

1. Which Eagle scored on the famous 1978 play known as the 'Miracle at the Meadowlands'?

2. Who is the only Eagle to have won the NFL Defensive Player of the Year Award?

3. Which former wide receiver is the color-commentator on Eagles radio broadcasts?

4. The father of which 2017 Super Bowl-winning linebacker also played for the Eagles in 1985?

5. Which former Eagles great is the father of a world champion high jumper?

6. True or false – Donovan McNabb was the first player in NFL history to finish a season with 30 or more touchdown passes and fewer than 10 interceptions?

7. Which Super Bowl-winning head coach spent two seasons with the Eagles as a player (tight end) in 1967 and 1968?

8. Is the field at Lincoln Financial Field grass or artificial turf?

9. Did the Eagles have a winning or losing regular season record at Veterans Stadium?

10. Which Eagle's 94-yard pick six against the Jets in 1993 was described as "the greatest interception return in NFL history" by Steve Sabol from NFL Films?

11. Former head coach Doug Pederson was a quarterback with which four teams during his NFL playing career?

12. True or false – Eagles defensive star Vinny Curry is the brother of former Seattle linebacker Aaron Curry?

13. Did Andy Reid have a winning or losing record in playoff games with the Eagles?

14. In what year did the Eagles win their first NFL Championship?

15. Which team did they defeat 7-0 to win that first NFL crown?

16. The Eagles faced which team in the 1990 game that was dubbed the 'Pork Chop Bowl'?

17. After 13 years in Philadelphia Brian Dawkins spent the final three years of his NFL career with which team?

18. Which 2017 Super Bowl winner was originally selected by the Rams with the second overall pick of the 2008 NFL Draft?

19. Which of the following running backs amassed the most rushing yards while with the Eagles? a) Keith Byars b) Charlie Garner c) Herschel Walker

20. 'The Little Dictator' was the nickname of which Eagles coach? a) Chip Kelly b) Buddy Ryan c) Dick Vermeil

Quiz 11: Answers

1. Reggie White 2. Patrick Robinson 3. Derek Barnett 4. Mike Paterson 5. Jeremiah Trotter 6. Brian Dawkins 7. Troy Vincent and Eric Allen 8. Malcolm Jenkins 9. Jerome Brown 10. Andy Harmon 11. Trent Cole 12. Jason Babin 13. Eric Allen 14. James Willis and Troy Vincent 15. Brandon Graham and Derek Barnett 16. Fletcher Cox 17. Seth Joyner 18. Bill Bradley 19. c) Reggie White 20. b) 21

Quiz 13: Special Teams

1. Who is the Eagles' all-time leading points scorer?

2. Which kicker set the franchise record for the most points in a single season in 2014?

3. Who was the punter on the 2017 World Championship-winning team?

4. Up to the start of the 2021 season, who were the two Eagles with four punt return touchdowns?

5. Whose 107-yard kickoff return touchdown against the Titans in 2014 is the longest in franchise history?

6. In September 2017, Jake Elliott set the record for the longest field goal in team history. How long was that historic kick?

7. Elliott converted that record-breaking kick in a game against which division rival?

8. Which barefoot kicker was the previous holder of that record?

9. Which Eagles returner was the winning contestant on a 2011 episode of the TV gameshow 'Hole in the Wall'?

10. In 2012, who set a team record after converting 22 straight field goals?

11. True or false – No Eagles punter has ever been elected to the Pro Bowl?

12. Who was the long snapper on the Eagles 2017 Super Bowl team?

13. Whose 98-yard return for a touchdown against Dallas in 2012 is the longest punt return in team history?

14. In 2016, who set the franchise record for converting the most field goals in a season?

15. How many field goals did he successfully kick to set that record?

16. Which long-time NFL record holder holds the Eagles record for the most successful field goals in a game after booting six against Houston in 1972?

17. Who is the unlikely holder of the record for the longest punt in team history?

18. How long was that record-breaking boot?

19. What is the most points scored by an Eagles kicker in a single regular season? a) 148 b) 149 c) 150

20. Between 2004 and 2009 David Akers kicked how many straight extra points? a) 173 b) 183 c) 193

Quiz 12: Answers

1. Herm Edwards 2. Reggie White 3. Mike Quick 4. Najee Goode (father John) 5. Randall Cunningham 6. True 7. Mike Ditka 8. Grass 9. Winning 10. Eric Allen 11. Green Bay, Philadelphia, Miami and Cleveland 12. False 13. Losing 14. 1948 15. Chicago Cardinals 16. Dallas 17. Denver 18. Chris Long 19. a) Keith Byars 20. c) Dick Vermeil

Quiz 14: Pot Luck

1. In 2009, which Eagle tied the NFL record for the most 50-yard plus touchdowns in a single season with eight?

2. Who was the first Eagles running back to rush for over 1,000 yards in three straight seasons?

3. Which Hall of Fame receiver, best known for his 12 years in Minnesota, spent the first three years of his career with the Eagles?

4. Which Eagle won the NFL Comeback Player of the Year Award in 2010?

5. In October 2005, the Eagles turned a record 27-6 halftime deficit into a 37-31 victory over which AFC team?

6. True or false – Former Eagles kicker David Akers was born in England?

7. Which trio of running backs combined in 2003 for 1,618 rushing yards, 2,465 yards from scrimmage and 29 touchdowns?

8. Who holds the team record for scoring the most touchdowns in a single season?

9. How many touchdowns did he score to set that record?

10. Which defensive star scored his only receiving touchdown on a fake punt against the Texans in 2002?

11. True or false – The 33 points conceded by the Eagles in Super Bowl LII are the most by a winning team in Super Bowl history?

12. By what name was the Hall of Fame coach Earle Neale better known?

13. Which defensive stalwart scored his first career touchdown after scooping up a fumble and returning it 16 yards for a score against the Rams in December 2017?

14. Which Eagles linebacker was ejected from a 2005 game against Atlanta following a pregame scuffle with Kevin Mathis?

15. Did Andy Reid have a winning or losing record in his time with the Eagles?

16. Which Eagle set an NFL postseason record after scoring his fourth interception return touchdown in a January 2009 Wild Card game against the Vikings?

17. In what year did the Eagles play their first game at Veterans Stadium?

18. Who was the only Eagle elected to the NFL All-Decade Team of the 90s?

19. What was the nickname of former Eagles defensive back Andre Waters? a) Clear b) Dirty c) Still

20. What was the name of the center who went to three Pro Bowls in his four seasons with the Eagles in the 1960s? a) Jim Paul b) Jim George c) Jim Ringo

Quiz 13: Answers

1. David Akers 2. Cody Parkey 3. Donnie Jones 4. Darren Sproles and DeSean Jackson 5. Josh Huff 6. 61 yards 7. New York Giants 8. Tony Franklin 9. DeSean Jackson 10. Alex Henery 11. True 12. Rick Lovato 13. Damaris Johnson 14. Caleb Sturgis 15. 35 16. Tom Dempsey 17. Randall Cunningham 18. 91 yards 19. c) 150 20. a) 173

Quiz 15: 1980s

1. Which team did the Eagles face in Super Bowl XV?

2. What was the score in that game?

3. Which divisional rival did the Eagles beat to reach Super Bowl XV?

4. Who was the Eagles head coach at Super Bowl XV?

5. Which long-time defensive coordinator was appointed head coach in 1983?

6. Which kicker was named NFC Rookie of the Year in 1984?

7. Which quarterback's streak of 116 straight starts ended after he suffered broken leg against St. Louis in 1984?

8. Which businessman and car dealer became the team's new owner in April 1985?

9. Before becoming head coach in Philly Buddy Ryan had been the defensive coordinator at which Super Bowl-winning team?

10. In which round of the 1985 NFL Draft did the Eagles select quarterback Randall Cunningham?

11. Which wide receiver went to the Pro Bowl five times between 1983 and 1987?

12. True or false – In his rookie year Randall Cunningham threw just one touchdown and eight interceptions?

13. Which team did the Eagles face in the game known as 'The Fog Bowl'?

14. In December 1985, the Eagles blew a franchise record 23-point lead, eventually losing to which team 28-23?

15. Who were the two Eagles to rush for over 1,000 yards in a season during the 1980s?

16. Who were the two Eagles with over 1,000 receiving yards in a season during the 1980s?

17. How many division titles did the Eagles win during the 1980s?

18. Which defensive back led the NFC in interceptions in 1989 after picking off eight passes?

19. The 1989 Eagles defense holds the franchise record for the most sacks in a season after recording how many? a) 60 b) 61 c) 62

20. Despite his superb rushing talents, Randall Cunningham was sacked how many times in 1986? a) 52 b) 62 c) 72

Quiz 14: Answers

1. DeSean Jackson 2. Ricky Watters 3. Cris Carter 4. Michael Vick 5. Kansas City 6. False 7. Brian Westbrook, Correll Buckhalter and Duce Staley 8. LeSean McCoy 9. 20 touchdowns 10. Brian Dawkins 11. True 12. Greasy 13. Brandon Graham 14. Jeremiah Trotter 15. Winning 16. Asante Samuel 17. 1971 18. Reggie White 19. b) Dirty 20. c) Jim Ringo

Quiz 16: Pot Luck

1. Before moving to Veterans Stadiums, where did the Eagles play home games?

2. Who are the two Eagles head coaches to win the AP NFL Coach of the Year Award in the Super Bowl era?

3. Which versatile Eagle led the NFL in yards from scrimmage in 2007?

4. The Eagles won their third NFL title in 1960 after defeating which team 17-13 in the Championship game?

5. Which quarterback had more wins as a starter while with the Eagles – Rodney Peete or Michael Vick?

6. Which running back rushed for a touchdown in six straight games during the 1995 season?

7. Which Jacksonville Jaguar, who shares a name with a Hollywood legend, scored five rushing touchdowns against the Eagles in an October 1997 game?

8. Which Eagle returned an interception 102 yards for a touchdown against Dallas in October 2006?

9. Who was the only Eagle to start Super Bowl LII whose first name and surname start with the same letter?

10. True or false – Former Eagles tackle Jason Peters owns a Californian car shop called Greedy Boy Customs?

11. Which former Eagle co-wrote a book called 'Catch This - Going Deep With The NFL's Sharpest Weapon'?

12. Derek Barnett set the record for the most sacks at the University of Tennessee. Which Eagles great was the former holder of that record?

13. Which defensive back is best known for a brutal hit on Reggie Bush during the 2006 NFC Divisional Round Playoff?

14. Which Eagles defender was the winner of the NFLPA Byron 'Whizzer' White Award in 2017 for his charitable efforts off the field?

15. Which former Eagles linebacker unsuccessfully ran for the 1st Congressional District of New Jersey in a November 2014 election?

16. Which former Eagles offensive lineman was the incumbent congressman prior to that 2014 election?

17. Which defensive back picked off a pass in three straight games during the 2017 season?

18. True or false – Randall Cunningham is an ordained church minister?

19. Former head coach Doug Pederson started nine games for the Eagles at quarterback. How many of those games did Philly win? a) none b) one c) two

20. Which of the following quarterbacks had the most wins as a starter with the Eagles? a) Sam Bradford b) Jim McMahon c) Jeff Garcia

Quiz 15: Answers

1. Oakland 2. Raiders 27-10 Eagles 3. Dallas 4. Dick Vermeil 5. Marion Campbell 6. Paul McFadden 7. Ron Jaworski 8. Norman Braman 9. Chicago 10. Second 11. Mike Quick 12. True 13. Chicago 14. Minnesota 15. Wilbert Montgomery and Earnest Jackson 16. Mike Quick and Harold Carmichael 17. Two 18. Eric Allen 19. c) 62 20. c) 72

Quiz 17: 1990s

1. Buddy Ryan was fired as head coach following a 20-6 wild card loss to which division rival?

2. Which former offensive coordinator became the team's 18th head coach in January 1991?

3. Which three Eagles defensive linemen on the 1991 team were elected to the Pro Bowl that season?

4. The 1992 Eagles won their first playoff game in more than a decade, defeating which then NFC West team 36-20 in the wild card round?

5. In 1994, which Eagle became the first player in NFL history to record a 90-yard plus run, reception and kick return in the same season?

6. Which rookie running back rushed for over 100 yards in his first two appearances for the Eagles in 1994?

7. Which receiver's 95-yard touchdown catch against the Bills in 1990 is the second longest in Eagles history?

8. Which alliteratively named former 49ers defensive coordinator become the Eagles head coach in 1995?

9. Which quarterback steered the 1995 Eagles to wins in nine of their final 12 games and a playoff berth?

10. Which team did the Eagles defeat 58-37 in a crazy 1995 Wild Card game?

11. Which running back's 1,411 yards and 14 touchdowns in 1996 earned him a second straight Pro Bowl appearance?

12. Which defensive end recorded 35.5 sacks in a three-year spell in Philadelphia between 1994 and 1996?

13. The Eagles' final playoff appearance of the 1990s was a 14-0 Wild Card loss to which team in 1996?

14. The Eagles played out a single tied game in the 1990s, sharing a 10-10 scoreline with which AFC team in 1997?

15. Before becoming the head coach of the Eagles Andy Reid was the quarterbacks coach with which team?

16. The first draft pick of the Andy Reid era was used to select which future star?

17. Which running back accounted for 41% of the team's offense during the 1999 season?

18. Which Eagle tied for the NFL-lead in interceptions in 1999 after picking off seven passes?

19. How many NFC East titles did the Eagles win during the 1990s? a) none b) one c) two

20. How many games did the Eagles win in Andy Reid's first season in charge? a) four b) five c) six

Quiz 16: Answers

1. Franklin Field 2. Ray Rhodes and Andy Reid 3. Brian Westbrook 4. Green Bay 5. Michael Vick 6. Ricky Watters 7. James Stewart 8. Lito Sheppard 9. Brandon Brooks 10. True 11. Terrell Owens 12. Reggie White 13. Sheldon Brown 14. Malcolm Jenkins 15. Garry Cobb 16. Jon Runyan 17. Rodney McLeod 18. True 19. c) Two 20. b) Jim McMahon

Quiz 18: Pot Luck

1. Before Doug Pederson, who was the last former Eagles player to return to the team as head coach?

2. Who was the only Eagle named on the First Team of the NFL All-Decade Team of the 2000s?

3. Which cornerback's 96-yard fumble return touchdown against Dallas in 2008 was the second longest in franchise history?

4. The #60 jersey has been retired in honor of which former linebacker and center?

5. The Eagles were involved in a rare tie in a 2008 game against which AFC North team?

6. What is the name of Jason Kelce's brother who plays tight end for the Chiefs?

7. Throughout their history which team have the Eagles beaten more times than any other?

8. In a wild 2007 game, the Eagles shared a record 62 first-half points with which NFC North team?

9. Which three 2017 World Champions had previously won a Super Bowl ring with the 2012 Ravens?

10. True or false – Rookie Carson Wentz won his first three games as a starter with the Eagles?

11. Who was the only Eagles quarterback elected to the Pro Bowl during the 1990s?

12. After leaving the Eagles, cornerback Jalen Mills joined which team?

13. True or false – Former Eagles offensive tackle Jason Peters is the older brother of Rams defensive back Marcus Peters?

14. In 2002, which Eagle became the first player in NFL history to intercept a pass, record a sack, force a fumble, and score a touchdown in the same game?

15. Which running back, who was with the Eagles from 1944 until 1951, was named on the NFL's 75th Anniversary Team?

16. The Eagles famously stopped which Dallas running back on fourth and one not once but twice in the closing stages of a memorable 1995 match up?

17. A multiple Pro Bowler with the Eagles, Troy Vincent started his NFL career with which team?

18. Safety Malcolm Jenkins spent the first five years of his NFL career with which team?

19. Which of the following receivers had the best yards per catch average with the Eagles? a) DeSean Jackson b) Jeremy Maclin c) Mike Quick

20. What is the official color of the Eagles home jersey? a) forest green b) meadow green c) midnight green

Quiz 17: Answers

1. Washington 2. Rich Kotite 3. Reggie White, Clyde Simmons and Jerome Brown 4. New Orleans 5. Herschel Walker 6. Charlie Garner 7. Fred Barnett 8. Ray Rhodes 9. Rodney Peete 10. Detroit 11. Ricky Watters 12. William Fuller 13. San Francisco 14. Baltimore 15. Green Bay 16. Donovan McNabb 17. Duce Staley 18. Troy Vincent 19. None 20. b) Five

Quiz 19: 2000s

1. True or false – The Eagles opened the 2000 season with a successfully converted onside kick?

2. Which team did the Eagles face in Super Bowl XXXIX?

3. What was the final score in that game?

4. Which city hosted Super Bowl XXXIX?

5. In what year did the Eagles play their first game at Lincoln Financial Field?

6. The Eagles were shut out 17-0 by which team in the first regular season game played at the Linc?

7. Philly defeated which division rival 27-25 to gain their maiden win at Lincoln Financial Field?

8. The Eagles opened their 2004 campaign by winning how many straight games?

9. In September 2007, the Eagles routed which NFC rival by a score of 56-21?

10. Which veteran quarterback was 5-1 as a starter in 2006 after taking over from the injured Donovan McNabb?

11. True or false – Before becoming head coach in Philadelphia Andy Reid had never held an offensive or defensive coordinator post?

12. The 2001 Eagles reached the NFC Championship Game for the first time in over 20 years, eventually losing 29-24 to which team?

13. The last game hosted at Veterans Stadium saw the Eagles lose 27-10 in an NFC Championship game against which team?

14. Which third string quarterback went 4-1 in his five starts at the end of the 2002 regular season?

15. Who returned a punt 84 yards for a game-winning-score to give the Eagles a late win over which division rival in October 2003?

16. Which team defeated the 2008 Eagles in the NFC Championship Game?

17. True or false – The Eagles didn't record a losing season throughout the whole of the 2000s?

18. Whose nine interceptions in 2009 put him tied second on the Eagles' most picks in a season list?

19. What was the most games won by the Eagles in a single regular season in the 2000s? a) 11 b) 12 c) 13

20. In road games in 2001 the Eagles defense allowed how many points? a) 64 b) 74 c) 84

Quiz 18: Answers

1. Marion Campbell 2. Brian Dawkins 3. Joselio Hanson 4. Chuck Bednarik 5. Cincinnati 6. Travis 7. New York Giants 8. Detroit 9. Corey Graham, Torrey Smith and Dannell Ellerbe 10. True 11. Randall Cunningham 12. New England 13. False 14. Brian Dawkins 15. Steve Van Buren 16. Emmitt Smith 17. Miami 18. New Orleans 19. c) Mike Quick 20. c) Midnight green

Quiz 20: Pot Luck

1. Which Eagle gave a memorable, profanity-filled speech, while wearing a Mummers costume during the Super Bowl LII parade?

2. Which offensive lineman did the Eagles select with the fourth overall pick of the 2013 NFL Draft?

3. Which Eagles cornerback was the winner of the NFL Walter Payton Man of the Year Award in 2002?

4. Who was the last head coach before Doug Pederson to steer the team to a playoff berth?

5. The Eagles sent a fifth-round draft pick to which team to acquire the services of Darren Sproles?

6. Who are the three quarterbacks to have played in over 100 games for the Eagles?

7. Kicker Jake Elliott was originally drafted by which AFC team?

8. True or false – In a 1965 game against Pittsburgh the Eagles defense picked off nine passes?

9. Which safety played in 92% of the team's snaps in 2017, the most by a defensive player?

10. Up to the start of the 2021 season did the Eagles have a winning or losing playoff record?

11. Running back Jay Ajayi was born in which European capital city?

12. What color is the Eagles helmet?

13. Which Eagles running back passed 1,000 rushing yards in a season for the first time in 2006?

14. True or false – Legendary Eagles running back Steve Van Buren was born in the central American country Honduras?

15. Which Eagles defensive star is the owner of his own drag racing team?

16. Whose 1,169 points were the most scored by any player in the NFL in the 2000s?

17. Which running back's 93-yard catch against the Giants in 1994 is the longest reception in team history that didn't result in a touchdown?

18. In a 2014 game against the Giants, the Eagles wore what color shirt and pants combination for the first time?

19. In what year did the Eagles replace their famous Kelly-green jerseys? a) 1986 b) 1996 c) 2006

20. The parking lot at the Linc has spaces for how many cars? a) 22,000 b) 24,000 c) 26,000

Quiz 19: Answers

1. True 2. New England 3. Patriots 24-21 Eagles 4. Jacksonville 5. 2003 6. Tampa Bay 7. Washington 8. Seven games 9. Detroit 10. Jeff Garcia 11. True 12. St Louis Rams 13. Tampa Bay 14. A.J. Feeley 15. Brian Westbrook 16. Arizona 17. False 18. Asante Samuel 19. c) 13 20. a) 64

Quiz 21: 2010s

1. In a 2010 game against the Giants, which Eagle became the first player in NFL history to return a punt for a game-winning touchdown as time expired?

2. Which Eagles quarterback was elected to the Pro Bowl after a successful 2010 season?

3. Which defensive line duo combined for 29 sacks during the 2011 season?

4. Before becoming head coach of the Eagles, Chip Kelly had a successful spell in charge of which college team?

5. Which linebacker's 14.5 sacks in 2014 were the most in the NFC?

6. The Eagles scored a record 28 fourth quarter points to seal a stunning victory against which divisional foe in December 2010?

7. In 2014, two Eagles returned kickoffs over 100 yards for a touchdown. Josh Huff was one. Which running back was the other?

8. In November 2010 the Eagles scored a record 28 points in the first quarter of a game against which divisional rival?

9. Which Eagles kicker holds the record for the most points by a rookie in NFL history?

10. The 2013 Eagles suffered a heart-breaking 26-24 Wild Card round defeat to which team?

11. Which former number five overall pick was 4-6 as a starting quarterback with the Eagles in 2014 and 2015?

12. Which former NFL rushing title winner rushed for just 702 yards in his single season with the Eagles in 2015?

13. What was the Eagles' record in Chip Kelly's final season in Philadelphia?

14. Between 2010 and 2020 who was the only Eagle to rush for over 1,000 yards in a season?

15. Three different Eagles receivers caught over 80 passes in 2013, 2014 and 2015. Name the trio.

16. Which two Eagles, both on offense, were named First-Team All-Pros in both 2011 and 2013?

17. In October 2011, the Eagles blew a 20-point lead to lose 24-23 to which NFC West team?

18. Which Eagle led the NFL in most interceptions by a linebacker in 2016?

19. Andy Reid's final playoff game with the Eagles resulted in a 21-16 Wild Card loss to which team? a) Dallas b) Green Bay c) New York Giants

20. How many points did the Eagles give up in Andy Reid's final season in charge? a) 424 b) 434 c) 444

Quiz 20: Answers

1. Jason Kelce 2. Lane Johnson 3. Troy Vincent 4. Chip Kelly 5. New Orleans 6. Donovan McNabb, Randall Cunningham and Ron Jaworski 7. Cincinnati 8. True 9. Malcolm Jenkins 10. Winning 11. London 12. Green 13. Brian Westbrook 14. True 15. Fletcher Cox 16. David Akers 17. Herschel Walker 18. All black 19. b) 1996 20. a) 22,000

Quiz 22: Pot Luck

1. In what year did the Eagles play their first ever game?

2. Before Carson Wentz in October 2017, who was the last Eagle to win the NFC Player of the Month Award?

3. Before being appointed head coach of the Eagles, Dick Vermeil was a Rose Bowl-winner with which college?

4. What is the name of the Eagles mascot?

5. Which offensive lineman appeared in 1,079 of the team's 1,131 snaps during the 2017 regular season?

6. True or false – Ron Jaworksi was never elected to the Pro Bowl?

7. Which Eagle is married to the World Cup-winning soccer star Julie Johnston?

8. Which safety's streak of 159 consecutive regular season appearances ended against the Giants in September 2017?

9. How many games did the Eagles win in Andy Reid's final season as head coach?

10. Which Hall of Famer's number 15 jersey number has been retired by the Eagles?

11. True or false – Reggie White recorded double-digit sacks in each of his eight seasons in Philadelphia?

12. Who was the last Eagles head coach to have an overall losing record?

13. 'Concrete Charlie' was the nickname of which versatile Eagle?

14. Who were the three Eagles to rush for over 1,000 yards in a season during the 1990s?

15. True or false – The Eagles finished bottom of the NFC East the season before they won their first Super Bowl?

16. In 2015, the Eagles acquired the services of Sam Bradford following a trade with which team?

17. Who was the only Eagles defender to be named on the NFL's 75th Anniversary Team?

18. 'Green Goblin' is the nickname of which former Eagles defender?

19. What was the nickname of the 1960s Pro Bowl lineman Bob Brown? a) The Bouncer b) The Boomer c) The Bumper

20. How tall was star receiver Harold Carmichael? a) 6ft 4in b) 6ft 6in c) 6ft 8in

Quiz 21: Answers

1. DeSean Jackson 2. Michael Vick 3. Jason Babin and Trent Cole 4. Oregon 5. Conor Barwin 6. New York Giants 7. Chris Polk 8. Washington 9. Cody Parkey 10. New Orleans 11. Mark Sanchez 12. DeMarco Murray 13. 7-9 14. LeSean McCoy 15. DeSean Jackson, Jeremy Maclin and Jordan Matthews 16. LeSean McCoy and Jason Peters 17. San Francisco 18. Jordan Hicks 19. a) Green Bay 20. c) 444

Quiz 23: Numbers Game

Identify the jersey number worn by the following Eagles.

1. Nick Foles and Rodney Peete

2. Trent Cole and Jordan Hicks

3. Ron Jaworski and Michael Vick

4. Jay Ajayi and Brian Westbrook

5. Tommy McDonald and LeSean McCoy

6. Jalen Mills and Wilbert Montgomery

7. Zach Ertz and Fred Barnett

8. Clyde Simmons and Derek Barnett

9. Harold Carmichael and Alshon Jeffery

10. Brian Mitchell and Charlie Garner

11. Mike Quick and Torrey Smith

12. Kevin Kolb and Jake Elliott

13. Trey Burton and Keith Jackson

14. Patrick Robinson and Eric Allen

15. Asante Samuel and Brandon Boykin

16. Jason Babin and Beau Allen

17. Bill Bradley and Correll Buckhalter

18. Hugh Douglas and Nigel Bradham

19. Irving Fryar and Kevin Curtis

20. Alex Henery and Caleb Sturgis

Quiz 22: Answers

1. 1933 2. LeSean McCoy 3. UCLA 4. Swoop 5. Jason Kelce 6. False 7. Zach Ertz 8. Corey Graham 9. Four 10. Steve Van Buren 11. True 12. Ray Rhodes 13. Chuck Bednarik 14. Ricky Watters, Duce Staley and Herschel Walker 15. True 16. St Louis Rams 17. Reggie White 18. Jalen Mills 19. b) The Boomer 20. c) 6ft 8in

Quiz 24: Pot Luck

1. Who was the last Eagles tight end before Zach Ertz to be voted to the Pro Bowl?

2. When the Eagles traded LeSean McCoy to Buffalo which linebacker moved in the opposite direction?

3. Who won his only game as the Eagles interim head coach in the final game of the 2015 season?

4. How many games did the Eagles win in Doug Pederson's first season as head coach?

5. 'The Dutchman' was the nickname of which quarterback who led the Eagles to the NFL Championship title in 1960?

6. True or false – During World War II the Eagles temporarily merged with Pittsburgh to form a team called the Steagles?

7. Who were the two Eagles backs to rush for over 1,000 yards in a season during the 2000s?

8. Which linebacker and special teams ace took over kickoff duties against Dallas in November 2017 after an injury to Jake Elliott?

9. Quarterback Donovan McNabb played college ball at which school?

10. Who holds the franchise record for the most successful field goals of 50 yards or more in a single season?

11. True or false – The Eagles never finished in last place in their division during the Andy Reid era?

12. Multiple Pro Bowl offensive lineman Jason Peters wore what number jersey?

13. True or false – MLB MVP Mike Trout is an Eagles season ticket holder?

14. Running back Duce Staley wore what number jersey?

15. Which rookie Eagles linebacker returned a Matt Cassell pass 67 yards for a touchdown against Dallas in November 2015?

16. Who holds the team record for the most receiving yards in playoff games?

17. Randall Cunningham spent the majority of his career with the Eagles but also had spells with which three other teams?

18. True or false – A Pennsylvania brewery released a special beer in honor of Jason Kelce's memorable Super Bowl parade speech?

19. The Eagles entered the NFL after the demise of which franchise? a) Frankford Green Jackets b) Frankford Red Jackets c) Frankford Yellow Jackets

20. What is the most yards the Eagles have rushed for in a single game? a) 276 b) 326 c) 376

Quiz 23: Answers

1. #9 2. #58 3. #7 4. #36 5. #25 6. #31 7. #86 8. #96 9. #17 10. #30 11. #82 12. #4 13. #88 14. #21 15. #22 16. #94 17. #28 18. #53 19. #80 20. #6

Quiz 25: Anagrams

Rearrange the letters to make the name of a current or former Eagles player or coach.

1. Nose Flick

2. Underdog Pose

3. Drops Learners

4. Czar Won Nest

5. Van Con And Bomb

6. Razz Tech

7. Same Cyclone

8. Neck Treble

9. Crochet Flex

10. Dye Drain

11. Rabid Swan Ink

12. Jars Iron Wok

13. Pets Or Jeans

14. Colt Enter

15. Borrows Beatnik

16. Armchair Held Coal

17. Sacked Jeans On

18. Advised Ark

19. Jason Kelce

20. Honors Galleon

Quiz 24: Answers

1. Chad Lewis 2. Kiko Alonso 3. Pat Shurmur 4. Seven 5. Norm Van Brocklin 6. True 7. Brian Westbrook and Duce Staley 8. Kamu Grugier-Hill 9. Syracuse 10. Jake Elliott 11. False 12. #71 13. True 14. #22 15. Jordan Hicks 16. Harold Carmichael 17. Minnesota, Dallas and Baltimore 18. True 19. c) Frankford Yellow Jackets 20. c) 376

Bonus Questions

Bonus Questions: Quiz 1

1. Which legendary Eagles was inducted into the Pro Football Hall of Fame in August 2021?

2. Who holds the franchise record for the most yards from scrimmage in a single season?

3. Philadelphia's Travis Kelce holds the NFL record for the most catches in a season by a tight end. Who was the previous holder of that record?

4. Whose 175 games played between 2007 and 2017 are the most by an Eagles tight end?

5. Excluding current divisional opponents which team have the Eagles defeated the most times throughout their history?

6. What number jersey does wide receiver DeVonta Smith wear?

7. Do the Eagles have a winning or losing record in the NFC Championship Game?

8. In 2020, Jalen Hurts became just the fourth quarterback in NFL history to pass for 300+ yards and rush for 60+ yards twice in a season. Who are the other three quarterbacks to do so?

9. Who holds the franchise record for the most rushing yards by an Eagles rookie?

10. Who was the only Eagles defender named on the NFL's 2010's All Decade Team?

11. True or false – Tight end Dallas Goedert is an accomplished unicyclist?

12. The longest pass reception in a playoff game was a 76-yard touchdown against the Cowboys in January 2010. Who caught it?

13. Which quarterback threw that record long postseason pass?

14. Who returned a Tom Brady interception 99 yards for a touchdown in a December 2015 game against the Patriots?

15. Which alliteratively named quarterback threw 16 TD passes for the Eagles in 1993 and 1994 and later won a Super Bowl ring with Denver?

16. Who was the longest tenured player on the Eagles 2021 roster?

17. In 2020, the Eagles sent 3rd and 5th round draft picks to which team to acquire the services of cornerback Darius Slay?

18. Which Eagles o-lineman had a job as a grave digger while at high school?

19. With which pick of the 1999 NFL Draft did the Eagles select quarterback Donovan McNabb? a) First b) Second c) Third

20. Jalen Hurts threw hist first career TD pass to which receiver? a) Zach Ertz b) Travis Fulgham c) Greg Ward

Bonus Quiz 5 Answers

1. Brandon Brooks, Lane Johnson and Jason Kelce 2. Jalen Reagor 3. Darren Sproles 4. Alex Singleton 5. 10th 6. Silver Linings Playbook 7. David Akers 8. Herman Edwards 9. Return a punt for a touchdown 10. Houston Texans 11. Brandon Graham 12. Winning 13. Donovan McNabb 14. Temple 15. Kurt Coleman 16. True 17. Nick Foles 18. LeSean McCoy 19. a) Aussie Rules Football 20. c) Spain

Bonus Questions: Quiz 2

1. Which Eagles defender was named to the Pro Bowl for the first time after registering eight sacks during the 2020 season?

2. Immediately prior to becoming the head coach in Philadelphia, Nick Sirianni had been the offensive coordinator at which AFC team?

3. In which round of the 2020 NFL Draft did the Eagles select quarterback Jalen Hurts?

4. Which Eagles offensive lineman was named on the NFL's 2010s All Decade Team?

5. Who tied a franchise record after rushing for three touchdowns in a December 2019 win over the Giants?

6. Which Heisman Trophy winner did the Eagles select in the 2021 NFL Draft?

7. Who are the three Eagles quarterbacks with more than 20,000 passing yards?

8. The Eagles traded Carson Wentz to which team?

9. Whose 82-yard touchdown run against the Saints in December 2020 is the fourth longest in franchise history?

10. Which defensive tackle returned a fumble for a franchise record 98-yard touchdown in a September 2006 game against the 49ers?

11. Which tight end holds the franchise record for the most catches in playoff games?

12. Which current AFC team have the Eagles defeated the most times in franchise history?

13. Do the Eagles have an all-time winning or losing record in primetime games?

14. In week 16 of the 2020 season, Jalen Hurts threw an 81-yard touchdown pass to which receiver?

15. Before being named as Philadelphia's offensive coordinator in 2021, Shane Steichen had been in the same position with which AFC team?

16. Rearrange the letters Sends Mailers and you'll get the name of which Eagles offensive star?

17. Which Eagles o-lineman's pre-game routine includes listening to Christmas songs?

18. Which Super Bowl MVP joined the Eagles as a backup quarterback in 2021?

19. Who holds the franchise record for the most touchdown receptions in playoff games? a) Harold Carmichael b) Brent Celek c) Alshon Jeffery

20. Who is the only Eagle with 400+ touches in a single season? a) LeSean McCoy b) Duce Staley c) Ricky Watters

Bonus Quiz 1 Answers

1. Harold Carmichael 2. LeSean McCoy 3. Jason Witten 4. Brent Celek 5. Cardinals 6. #6 7. Losing 8. Steve Young, Michael Vick and Russell Wilson 9. Miles Sanders 10. Fletcher Cox 11. True 12. Jeremy Maclin 13. Michael Vick 14. Malcolm Jenkins 15. Bubby Brister 16. Brandon Graham 17. Detroit 18. Lane Johnson 19. b) Second 20. c) Greg Ward

Bonus Questions: Quiz 3

1. Who was appointed Philadelphia's defensive coordinator for the 2021 season?

2. Quarterback Jalen Hurts played for which two college teams?

3. Which Eagles kicker holds the NFL record for the longest field goal by a rookie?

4. Which special teamer was elected to his first Pro Bowl after a stellar 2019 season?

5. Who holds the franchise record for the most career sacks by an Eagles defensive tackle?

6. Which linebacker returned a Nick Mullens interception 30 yards for a touchdown in an October 2020 Sunday Night Football win over the 49ers?

7. How many games did the Eagles win in Doug Pederson's final season as head coach?

8. Before Jalen Hurts, who was the last Eagles quarterback to enjoy a 100-yard rushing game?

9. Whose 262 yards from scrimmage in a September 2000 game against Dallas are the most in team history?

10. Who are the two Eagles to have topped 1,000 yards from scrimmage in their rookie season?

11. Who is Philadelphia's all-time leading rusher in playoff games?

12. Who holds the franchise record for scoring the most rushing touchdowns in playoff games?

13. The Eagles have a perfect 4-0 record in playoff games against which opponent?

14. The Eagles used their first two picks in the 2021 NFL Draft to select players from which college?

15. Philadelphia set an NFL record in 2019 after registering 10 sacks, a fumble return TD and an interception return TD against which opponent?

16. Jalen Hurts wore what number jersey in his rookie season?

17. Hurts changed that number in his second season to what?

18. Only one tight end in NFL history has reached 500 catches in fewer games than Travis Kelce. Which tight end?

19. In a December 2018 game at Washington, Nick Foles tied an NFL record after completing how many consecutive passes? a) 24 b) 25 c) 26

20. David Akers holds the team record for the most consecutive extra points converted with how many? a) 153 b) 163 c) 173

Bonus Quiz 2 Answers

1. Brandon Graham 2. Indianapolis 3. Second 4. Jason Peters 5. Boston Scott 6. DeVonta Smith 7. Donovan McNabb, Ron Jaworski and Randall Cunningham 8. Indianapolis 9. Miles Sanders 10. Mike Patterson 11. Chad Lewis 12. Pittsburgh 13. Winning 14. DeSean Jackson 15. L.A. Chargers 16. Miles Sanders 17. Jason Kelce 18. Joe Flacco 19. a) Harold Carmichael 20. c) Ricky Watters

Bonus Questions: Quiz 4

1. Who became the first Eagles wide receiver since 1990 to score a touchdown in his NFL debut in the 2021 season opener against Atlanta?

2. Which Eagles receiver was an intern for former Secretary of State Condoleezza Rice while at college at Stanford?

3. True or false – In a 2017 game against the Giants, the Eagles blocked a punt, a field goal and an extra point?

4. In 2020, who became the first wide receiver since Terrell Owens to catch touchdown passes in each of his first three appearances for the Eagles?

5. Who is the only Eagle to rush for multiple 70+ yard touchdowns in the same season?

6. In September 2020, the Eagles were involved in their first tie in 12 years, sharing a 23-23 scoreline with which AFC opponent?

7. Who holds the record for the most games played by an Eagles wide receiver?

8. Which quarterback holds the franchise record for the most passing yards in a single game with 471?

9. Whose 14 catches against Dallas in November 2007 are the most in a single game by an Eagles running back?

10. In a 1998 game at San Diego, which defensive end tied a franchise record after registering 4.5 sacks?

11. Which defensive tackle's 9.5 sacks in 2000 are the most in franchise history by an Eagles rookie?

12. Which defensive back picked off a franchise record five passes in just seven postseason games in the late 1970s and early 1980s?

13. Which versatile Eagle led the team in both rushing and receiving in a December 2019 game at the New York Giants?

14. What was special about Philadelphia's 23-17 win over Atlanta on 10 November 1985?

15. Who was the first coach to steer the Eagles to the playoffs following the 1970 AFL/NFL merger?

16. Before Jalen Reagor in 2020, who was the last wide receiver selected by the Eagles with their first pick in the NFL Draft?

17. Who had a better regular season win percentage as head coach of the Eagles – Chip Kelly or Doug Pederson?

18. 'Dogs Lateraled' is an anagram of which Eagles offensive player?

19. In which country was tackle Jordan Mailata born? a) Australia b) New Zealand c) Samoa

20. Before becoming an NFL kicker, Jake Elliott had enjoyed great success at youth level at which sport? a) Bowling b) Golf c) Tennis

Bonus Quiz 3 Answers

1. Jonathan Gannon 2. Alabama and Oklahoma 3. Jake Elliott 4. Rick Lovato 5. Fletcher Cox 6. Alex Singleton 7. Four 8. Michael Vick 9. Duce Staley 10. Miles Sanders and DeSean Jackson 11. Brian Westbrook 12. Wilbert Montgomery 13. Minnesota 14. Alabama 15. New York Jets 16. #2 17. #1 18. Kellen Winslow 19. b) 25 passes 20. c) 173

Bonus Questions: Quiz 5

1. Which three Eagles offensive lineman received Pro Bowl recognition in 2019?

2. Which rookie returned a punt 73 yards for a touchdown in a December 2020 game at Green Bay?

3. Which former Eagle holds the NFL record for the most all-purpose yards in a single season?

4. Before joining the Eagles in 2019, which defensive star spent three seasons with the CFL's Calgary Stampeders?

5. With which pick of the 2021 NFL Draft did the Eagles select receiver DeVonta Smith?

6. The Eagles featured heavily in which 2012 Academy Award-nominated movie starring Jennifer Lawrence and Bradley Cooper?

7. Who holds the team record for the most appearances in playoff games?

8. Which former Philly defensive back wrote a book called, 'You Play to Win the Game: Leadership Lessons for Success On and Off the Field'?

9. In a 1947 game against the Steelers, Bosh Pritchard became the first and so far, only Eagle to do what in a playoff game?

10. Up to the starts of the 2021 season, the Eagles were a perfect 5-0 in games against which opponent?

11. Who holds the franchise record for the most games played by an Eagles defensive lineman?

12. Do the Eagles have a winning or losing record in home playoff games?

13. Whose six Pro Bowl selections are the most for an Eagles quarterback?

14. What university team plays its home games at Lincoln Financial Field?

15. Which defensive back, who spent five seasons in Philadelphia, intercepted three passes in a single game against Washington in October 2011?

16. True or false – Kenneth Gainwell and Fletcher Cox are cousins?

17. Which quarterback holds the franchise record for the most games with 400 or more passing yards?

18. Who holds the franchise record for the most career touches by an Eagles player?

19. Before becoming a football player punter Arryn Siposs had been a professional at which sport? a) Aussie Rules Football b) Rugby c) Soccer

20. Wide receiver J.J. Arcega-Whiteside was born in which European country? a) France b) Portugal c) Spain

Bonus Quiz 4 Answers

1. DeVonta Smith 2. J.J. Arcega-Whiteside 3. True 4. Travis Fulgham 5. Miles Sanders 6. Cincinnati 7. Harold Carmichael 8. Nick Foles 9. Brian Westbrook 10. Hugh Douglas 11. Corey Simon 12. Herman Edwards 13. Boston Scott 14. It was the team's first overtime win 15. Dick Vermeil 16. Nelson Agholor 17. Chip Kelly 18. Dallas Goedert 19. a) Australia 20. c) Tennis

Made in the USA
Las Vegas, NV
15 December 2021

37831427R00039